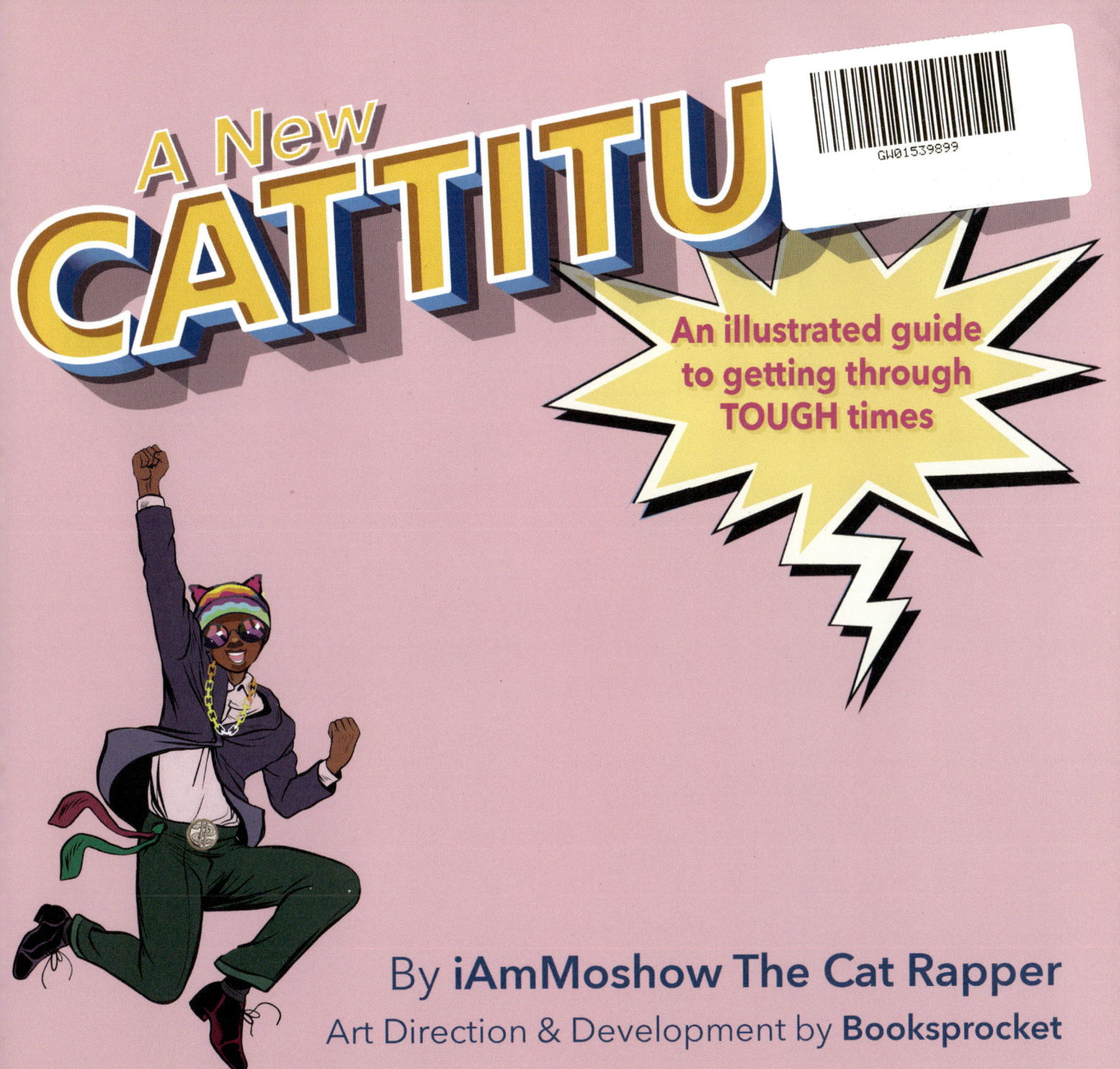

Text and illustrations
c 2020 iAmMoshow LLC

By iAmMoshow The Cat Rapper
Art Direction & Development by Booksprocket

All rights reserved. No part of this book may be reproduced or transmitted in any form or by any means, electronic or mechanical, including photocopying, recording, or by any information and retrieval system without permission from the publisher.

www.iAmMoshow.com

INTRODUCTION

I am a black man who raps about cats, sharing a message of love, joy, peace and acceptance. I don't check all of the boxes for what is considered acceptable behavior from a rapper, but I am not afraid of being myself. Years of hardship and failure strengthened my resolve and helped me become the fearless man I am today.

Fear can become a dark cloud that never leaves you alone, coloring every aspect of your life. It painted my early years, growing up in the projects as I watched my friends die one by one. I didn't know whether I would live past the age of sixteen, or if I would become just another statistic. Drugs and violence destroyed the lives of everyone around me, but I wanted to live.

The small voice inside my head is what kept me alive. It told me being different is not something to be ashamed of. The voice told me being unique is not something to fear. So instead of selling drugs I played video games. Instead of joining a gang I lived inside my head and dreamed about all of the things I could do to make my life different. While I grew into a man and my friends died, the fear that plagued me subsided when I realized surviving my childhood meant that I could truly survive anything.

Dr. Martin Luther King Jr. said, "all progress is precarious and the solution of one problem brings us face to face with another." Don't think for a moment I left all of my problems in my hometown. To this day I experience racism and indifference because of the color of my skin and my love for cats. But I persevere.

Spending so much time in my head has given me the opportunity to better understand myself, and to build a strategy for continued success. Over the years I've collected ideas from my song lyrics, little gems of wisdom from my notebooks, as well as my favorite inspirational quotes. Those ideas have grown with me and I am extremely proud to share them with you in this illustrated guide to getting through tough times.

Unfortunately hardship is part of the human experience, and as a society we are experiencing our fair share of hardship with the Covid-19 pandemic, political upheaval and economic challenges. It is my hope the ideas in this book will encourage you to look inward, and to feel empowered to develop a new CATTITUDE!

iAmMoshow

A NEW CATTITUDE

Stay True to Your Heart

Observe the Situation as an Outsider

Talk It Out

Don't Run from Change

Only Focus On the Things You CAN Control

Ditch Toxic People & Situations

Be Present with Yourself

Greet Each Day with Enthusiasm

Understand You Are Unique

STAY TRUE TO YOUR HEART

Sometimes the greatest moments of inspiration come in the quiet moments of the morning when everyone is asleep, and you are awake in bed with your heart in your hands. I've been where you are, and I know what it feels like to hit rock-bottom. Take some deep breaths and try to hit the pause button on all the chatter you hear in your brain. Use these few moments of silence to search inside yourself for the strength you will need to move forward. Answers will come in the silence, just listen.

OBSERVE THE SITUATION AS AN OUTSIDER

It is very easy to get caught up in the moment and lose perspective. Visualization exercises really work for me, and I truly believe much of my success in life is based on my ability to take an outsider's view. Hop on a flight in your imaginary hot air balloon, and watch your life unfold below. Pay close attention to all the details. Who do you see? What is their motivation? Can you see what's down the road, both figuratively and literally? If anything else, this exercise gives us a moment of pause before moving forward.

TALK IT OUT

I know I'm guilty of over-communicating my feelings at times, but I wear my emotions on my sleeve. I'm an artist and I draw upon my feelings to help guide me through life. It is the unspoken desires, unrequited love, and guarded secrets that keep us from getting what we want out of life. The problem with many over-communicators is they haven't taken the necessary steps to organize their thoughts and gain perspective of the situation they are facing. Reach out and talk to someone. You'll usually find someone willing to listen.

DON'T RUN FROM CHANGE

How easy is it to run for the hills and avoid responsibility when necessary changes are required? Humans (and cats) are such creatures of habit, we'd rather limp along than find a new solution. Change is inevitable. Change helps us navigate and adapt to a world that is in constant motion. So, once again, take those deep breaths and focus on the outcome you'd like to experience. If you want to feel better, think about feeling better. If you want to be more successful, think about being more successful. Life will soon begin to change.

ONLY FOCUS ON THE THINGS YOU CAN CONTROL

It's easy to feel trapped and helpless when we are consumed with all of the worry and doubt over what we can't do. What if you simply pivot and focus on what you can do instead? One thing leads to another, and sooner than later you'll realize there were solutions in front of you all along. I guarantee this is the best path forward because whatever decision you settle upon will be made with pawsitivity and an open-mind!

DITCH TOXIC PEOPLE & SITUATIONS

There is so much going on in our own minds, interactions with others can occasionally complicate matters... especially if they are toxic or counterproductive. You know in your heart if someone you are affiliated with makes moving forward difficult. They consistently place roadblocks in your path or come up with excuses to prevent you from making the decisions you need to make. Ditch them as soon as you can! You life will be so much easier once you do.

BE PRESENT WITH YOURSELF

There is evidence that mindfulness is important for your long term well-being. How you achieve a state of mindfulness is up to you, whether it's through meditation, prayer, or just going somewhere quiet to relax and think. Almost every one of the steps I'm presenting in this book require some form of self-reflection. Like I said, change can be difficult, but the reward is worth all of the effort. Take time to listen to the voice inside you, pointing you in the right direction.

GREET EVERY DAY WITH ENTHUSIASM

How you begin your day has a major impact on your productivity and peace of mind. Leap out of bed, throw open the curtains and let the light into your life. Sometimes I want to hit the "Snooze" button ten times before greeting the new day, but I know groggy and cranky Moshow will regret it later. Jumpstart your day by feeling refreshed, clean and well-nourished. Try and prove me wrong.

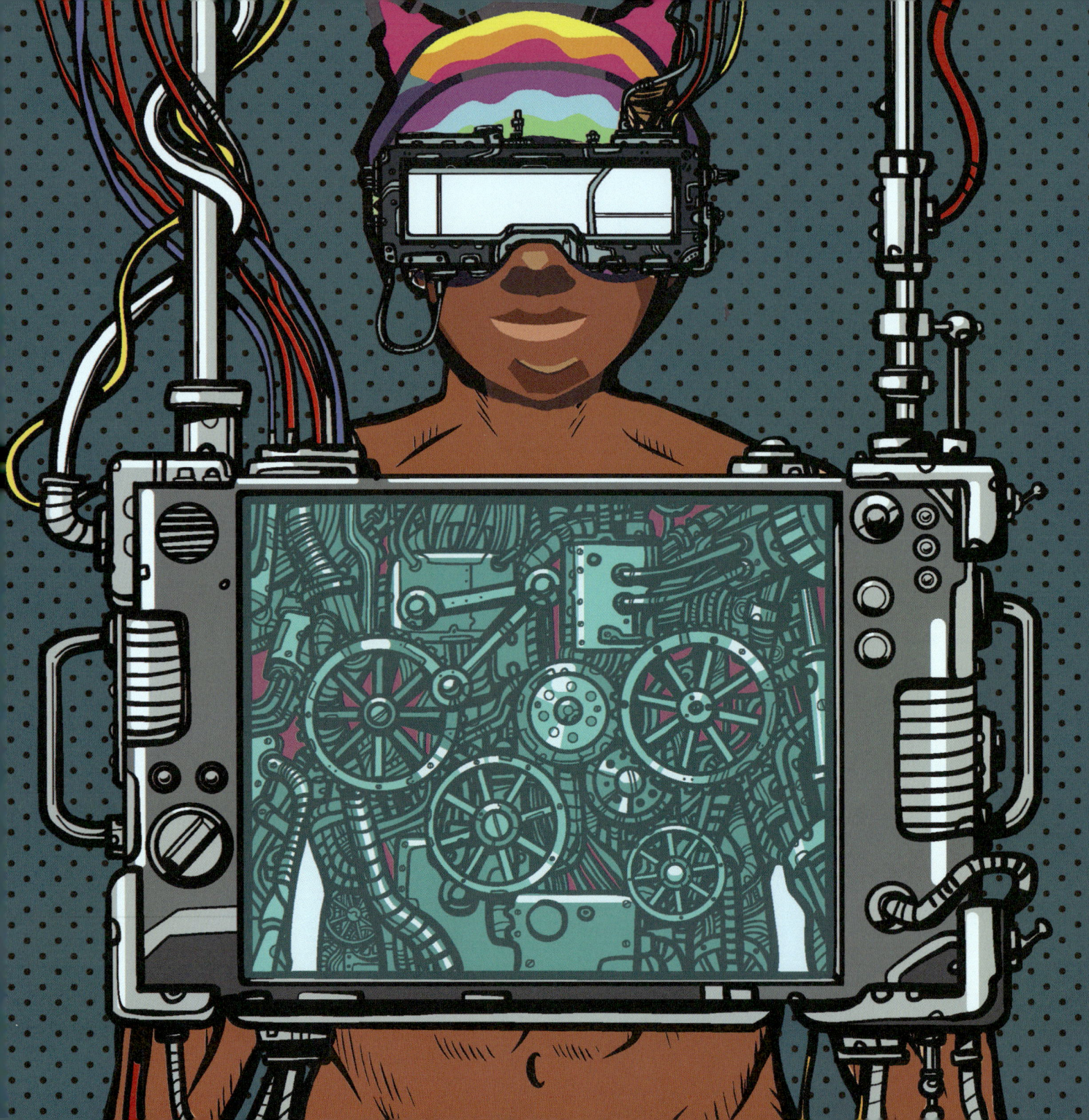

UNDERSTAND EVERYONE IS UNIQUE

News Flash, we are not robots! Each one of us is unique in how we approach situations, and how we recover from them as well. It's incredibly unproductive comparing ourselves to others, so why do we do it? It's human nature to seek the path of least resistance, plain and simple. However, if we take time to understand ourselves we'll eventually find our way when we are meant to do so. If you don't believe me, listen to The Byrds *"To everything there is a season, and a time to every purpose under heaven."* Turn, Turn, Turn.

MOVING FORWARD

There's no question about it, making positive changes in your life is difficult, especially if you are faced with significant hardships. Just know that each and every one of us has the power to make radical change if we look within. I've learned I can accomplish anything I want with the right mindset, and that has been a powerful tool in my life.

Right now there are a lot of unknowns in the world in relation to heath, politics, the economy, and so much more. It seems as if the world is in chaos. If you look to history as proof that society can overcome significant challenges, you'll see in most cases we are given an opportunity to learn and grow in the process.

I hope the tips I've provided in this book give you hope and inspire you to get through the challenges you face. I really do care about your well-being. In fact, I've added a few more tips on the following pages about healthy living, plus some resources for support if you need it.

Please don't doubt your potential. Just look within and you'll find you have the power to move mountains.

iAmMoshow

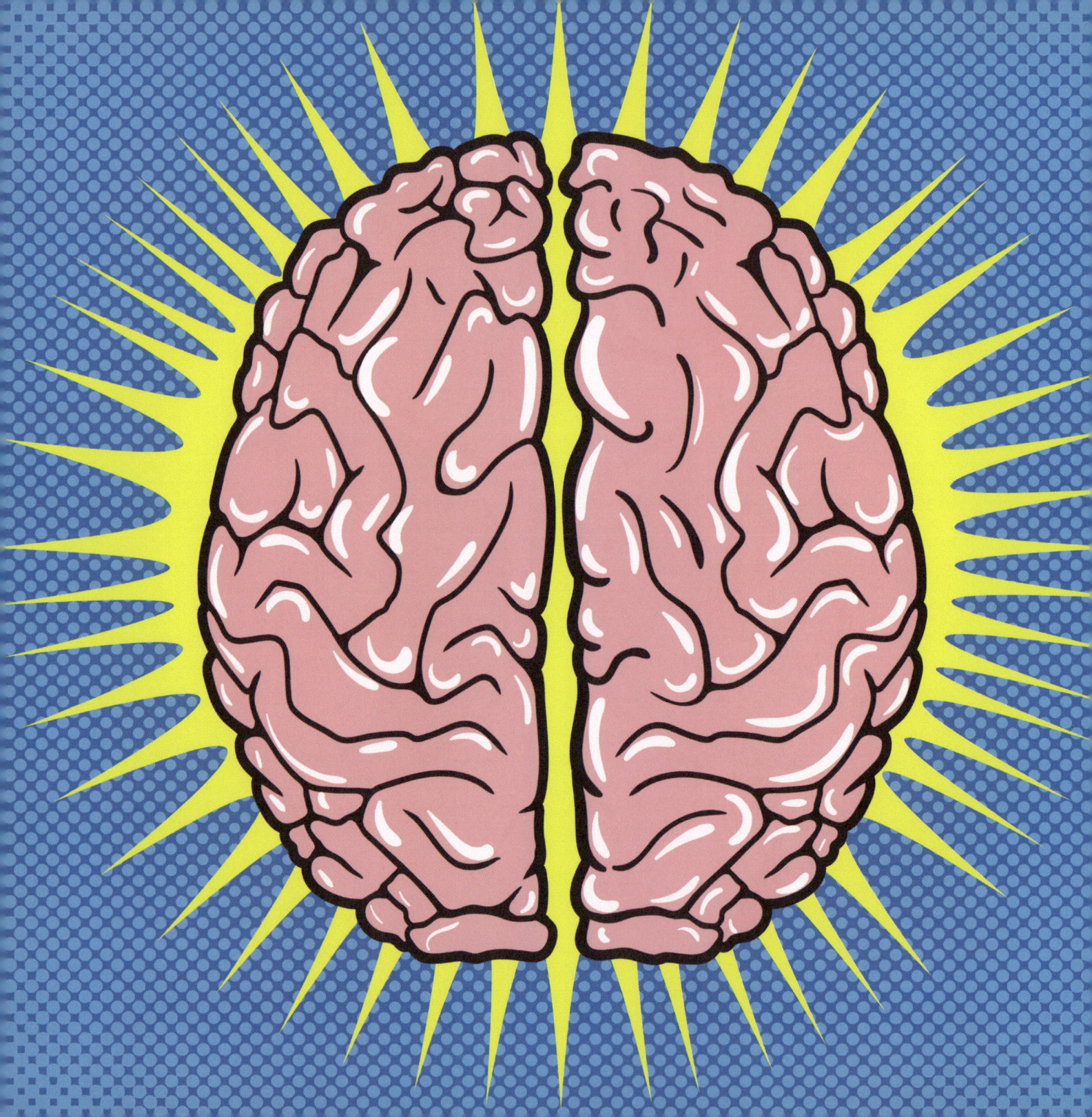

FEED YOUR BRAIN

Our bodies are machines that need maintenance in order to work effectively. I've made a commitment to fueling my brain so I can perform and create at peak levels, and I'm sharing some of those tips here with you.

Brain Food

I'm not a nutritionist, but I do know foods high in antioxidants keep my body healthy, and make me feel better. I run faster, think faster, and I am more creative. Research a Mediterranean diet for tips on how you can can improve your health.

- Leafy Green Veggies
- Berries
- Nuts
- Olive oil
- Whole grains
- Fish
- Beans
- Poultry

RELATIONSHIPS

I am the luckiest man alive to have found the person that accepts me for who I am, but also inspires me to improve and grow. My Cat Lady is everything I could ever hope for, but every relationship has room for growth. Here are some of the most important things we have learned.

- Accept and respect one another
- Take an active interest in each other's lives
- Give lots of emotional support and affection
- Work effectively together to solve problems
- Never go to bed angry
- It is important to have some similar Interests
- Admit when you are wrong
- Give each other space when we need it

These are the tips we found that work for us. Most importantly, I feel effective communication is the one thing that can help a relationship thrive and grow. If you can't talk things through, it's hard to imagine being able to make positive changes.

"I guess I'm proud that I kept on working, not becoming just a viral hit."
—Yung Lean

"Try to be a rainbow in someone's cloud."
—Maya Angelou

"The secret of life is enjoying the passage of time."— James Taylor

"Cause I think we can make it, in fact, I'm sure - And if you fall, stand tall and come back for more."
—Tupac

"Let us make our future now, and let us make our dreams tomorrow's reality."
—Malala Yousafzai

"I don't need it to be easy. I just want it to be worth it."
—Lil Wayne

"It matters not what someone is born, but what they grow to be." —J.K. Rowling

"I'm not a businessman, I'm a business, man!"
—Jay-Z

RESOURCES
for when the going gets tough

RESOURCES
for when the going gets tough

Coronavirus (Covid-19)

Centers for Disease Control and Prevention

This organization has a wealth of information about Covid-19 such as preventative measures, testing, and government updates regarding the pandemic. www.CDC.gov

The National Council for Behavioral Health

Information about tax incentives, loans and financial assistance. In addition, you will find information about tele-health services for medical and psychiatric assistance. www.thenationalcouncil.org/covid19

Feeding America

Feeding America and their network of food banks provide food to people in need during these times of uncertainty. More information can be found www.FeedingAmerica.org

National Council on Aging

Covid-19 resource center for older adults and caregivers affected by the worldwide pandemic www.NCOA.org

RESOURCES
for those suffering the loss of a cat

My Journal Entry from August 1st, 2019

HEART FAILURE. That night, both of our hearts stopped beating. Mine, just a few seconds. Tali's, forever. We lost her in the blink of an eye, with it all happening so fast it took me a minute to process everything. I'm gonna be real with you, losing Tali was one of the hardest things I've ever had to go through. And I grew up in the projects! For real, she was the love of my life.

For those of you who don't really know our story, Tali was the mother of my other cats MegaMan and Queen Sushi. She was the most lovable cat in the world. She was one of my ORIGINAL CREW, one of the first cats I ever had. She drove 3,000 miles with me cross country to our new home back when people were laughing at me and thought I was crazy. Before I was Moshow The Cat Rapper. It was just me, my Cat Lady and my kids in a new city.

Losing someone is never convenient. Life has been going really well with my music, with my books, and all the good things I'm trying to do. I keep having dreams about Tali, and it's like she's telling me to keep following my passion. The work is always a part of me, and my cats and Cat Lady have always been my inspiration. I just wanna make them happy and proud. We're in this together.

RESOURCES
for when the going gets tough

Anxiety, Depression and Mental Health Resources

800-273-TALK   **The National Suicide Prevention Lifeline**

The Lifeline provides 24/7, free and confidential support for people in distress, prevention and crisis resources for you or your loved ones.

800-950-NAMI   **National Alliance on Mental Illness**

NAMI is the largest grassroots organization devoted to improving the lives of those affected by mental illness.

240-485-1001   **Anxiety and Depression Association of America**

The programs of the nonprofit provides education, resources, and support for those affected by anxiety and depression looking to find treatment.

866-615-6464   **National Institute of Mental Health**

A research organization committed to understanding the treatment and prevention of mental disorders.

800-374-2721   **American Psychological Association**

The APA is a professional organization of psychologists. Its site explains how psychologists work with you to alleviate symptoms and offers information on how to manage health and well-being while coping with depression and anxiety.

RESOURCES
for when the going gets tough

Online Resources for dealing with Pet Loss

Association for Pet Loss and Bereavement
This website offers chat rooms and private counseling for those who are experiencing the loss of a pet. Their online catalog of resources is widely acknowledged as the best source of information and assistance for grieving animal lovers. www.aplb.org

Pet Loss Support Hotlines

877-474-3310   ASPCA Grief Counseling Line

855-352-5683   Lap of Love Pet Loss Support Hotline

607-253-3932   Cornell University Pet Loss Support Hotline

508-839-7966   Tufts University Pet Loss Support Hotline

866-266-8635   Washington State University Pet Loss Support

RESOURCES
for those suffering the loss of a cat

Kids Books About Pet Loss

Badger's Parting Gifts
Susan Varley, Lothrop, Lee and Shepard

Cat Heaven
Cynthia Rylant, Scholastic

For Every Cat an Angel
Christine Davis, Lighthearted Press

I'll Always Love You
Hans Wilhelm, Dragonfly Books

My Pet Died
Rachel Biale, Tricycle Press

Tear Soup
Pat Schwiebert & Chuck DeKlyen, Perinatal Loss

The Dead Bird
Margaret Brown, Harper Collins

The Rainbow Bridge: A Visit to Pet Paradise
Adrien Raeside, Harbour Publishing

When a Pet Dies
Fred Rogers, The Putnam and Grosset Group

About iAmMoshow The Cat Rapper

Born and raised in inner Baltimore, Maryland, Moshow defied the odds to build a name for himself as The Cat Rapper. He now calls Portland, Oregon his home with his 5 spirited cats - Black $avage, Sushi, Lil Parmesan, Mega Mam, and DJ Ravioli. *Visit iAmMoshow.com for more information.*

Printed in Poland
by Amazon Fulfillment
Poland Sp. z o.o., Wrocław